Craft Beer Revolution

A Guide to Launching Your Own Microbrewery

Table of Contents

Chapter 1. Introduction

In this enlightening Special Report, we delve into the heady world of craft beer – the Craft Beer Revolution, to be precise, that's swirling, fermenting, and bubbling in demijohns, and industrial vats around the world. This is your comprehensive guide to launching your very own microbrewery, a dream that bubbles in the heart of many a beer enthusiast. From hop selection and brewing techniques, to marketing strategies and navigating the legal landscape, we explore it all in an easy-to-grasp, matey way. This cheerful and accessible report is meant to inspire and guide you in turning your ale-infused dreams into reality. Given the booming craft beer industry, there's no better time to hop in! So, ready to stir the malt and brave the froth? Let this Special Report be your faithful guide on your exciting journey of launching a microbrewery.

Chapter 2. Understanding the Craft Beer Revolution

The craft beer revolution, as the name suggests, represents a seismic shift in the beer industry's landscape over the last few decades. It's a story of passionate brewers and avid consumers challenging the status quo and reshaping perceptions about beer.

2.1. Defining Craft Beer

The term "craft beer" may seem curious to those not intimately acquainted with the brewing world. It's typically associated with small and independent breweries that produce a relatively small quantity of beer. These breweries prioritize innovation, flavor, and traditional brewing methods.

According to the Brewers Association, a craft brewer must meet three distinct criteria:

1. Small: The annual production of craft beer must not exceed six million barrels.
2. Independent: Less than 25% of the brewery should be controlled by a beverage alcohol industry member.
3. Traditional: The brewer should make beers using traditional or innovative brewing ingredients.

Craft beer, thus, stands in direct contrast to mass-produced beers, which often favor efficiency and scale over taste and craftsmanship.

2.2. The Evolution of the Craft Beer Revolution

The roots of this revolution trace back to the 1970s in the United States when homebrewing was federally legalized. With groundbreaking innovators' efforts, an experimental culture took root, where brewing methods, styles, and ingredients were passionately tested. This wave spread, capturing the imagination and taste buds of countless beer lovers.

In the early days, pioneers like Jack McAuliffe and Ken Grossman dared to challenge the domination of mass-produced beer. These initial sparks ignited what we now label the Craft Beer Revolution.

The movement gained significant momentum in the 1990s and blossomed fully by the 21st century as 'craft' started carrying a cool, connoisseur choice zeitgeist. Today, beer drinkers worldwide appreciate the diverse spectrum of flavors and styles that craft beer offers.

2.3. The Marketplace and Growth

The craft beer revolution's economic impact is also striking as the industry now plays a significant role in the global beer market. Craft beer has experienced impressive growth that testifies its shift from novelty to mainstream.

According to Statista, the global craft beer market reached a value of approximately $98.3 billion in 2020 and is expected to grow further, reaching $160.5 billion by 2027.

Artisanal breweries provide local economies with jobs and contribute to community development. Bloomberg reports that, in 2018, the craft beer industry in the US contributed $79.1 billion to the national economy and created over 550,000 jobs.

2.4. Variety and Innovation: The Hallmark of Craft Beer

Another essential factor driving this revolution is the variety and innovation that craft brewing promises. The focus on quality ingredients and brewing methods has led to a veritable explosion of beer styles. From tangy sours and hoppy IPAs to robust stouts and Belgian ales, the choices are truly astounding. Craft brewers have been fearless in experimentation, incorporating a host of non-traditional ingredients like fruits, spices, and herbs into their brews.

Additionally, modern craft breweries often embody sustainability principles in their operations, championing the use of local products, implementing greener production methods, and fostering strong community relationships.

2.5. Changing Consumer Preferences

The craft beer boom can be partially attributed to shifts in consumer preferences. Today's beer enthusiast savors authenticity, a story behind the product, and values that align with their own. They appreciate knowing their beer's origin, the people who brewed it, and the craftsmanship that went into creating it.

This craving for a personalized, quality-focused beer experience is a cornerstone of the Craft Beer Revolution and is unlikely to dissipitalize soon.

In conclusion, understanding the Craft Beer Revolution is more than just understanding the shift in brewing methods and beer quality. It embodies understanding a cultural, societal, and economic transformation, driven by passionate brewers and appreciative consumers worldwide. This insightful journey prepares you, a future brewer, to grasp the industry's depth and height, setting your wheels in motion for the exciting venture ahead.

Chapter 3. Decoding the Beer Brewing Process

The brewing process is intricate, demanding equal parts art and science, patience and passion. From selecting the finest ingredients to the careful timing of each brewing phase, below is the process broken down in detail.

3.1. Choosing Your Ingredients

The first step is to gather your ingredients. Only four are essential: water, malt, hops, and yeast.

- **Water**: Around 90-95% of beer by volume, the quality of water has a considerable impact on the end product.
- **Malt**: One of the primary sources of beer's color, flavor, and sugar content (that later gets converted into alcohol).
- **Hops**: They provide the bitter, tangy taste that strikes a balance against the malt's sweetness.
- **Yeast**: This tiny fungus is the magical ingredient that ferments the beer's sugars, converting them into alcohol and carbon dioxide.

While these ingredients are foundational, supplemental ones like fruits, herbs, and spices may be added as per the desired beer style.

3.2. Mashing: Extracting the Sugars

Mashing is the process of combining crushed malt with hot water. Here, the hot water activates enzymes within the malt, which converts the residual starch into sugars - an essential step for fermentation. This mixture of water and malt, referred to as the 'mash', is then heated to 150-160 Fahrenheit over a period of 60-90 minutes. This temperature ensures the action of enzymes turning the bulk of starches into fermentable sugars.

The resulting mixture is known as 'wort' - sugar-rich water heading for fermentation.

3.3. Lautering: Separating the Wort from the Grain

The next step, lautering, involves separating the wort from the spent grain. The grain bed serves as a natural filter as the wort is drained through a process called 'vorlauf.' Re-circulation may occur until the wort is clear of grain particles. This can take an hour or two, but patience results in a pure, high-quality wort.

3.4. Boiling and Hop Addition

The wort is then taken into a pot for boiling, usually lasting around 60 minutes. Boiling has three crucial roles:

1. Sterilization: Destroys any remaining microorganisms.
2. Hops Infusion: Hops are added for bitterness, aroma, and preservation.
3. Water Reduction: Allows concentration of the wort.

Hops may be added at different phases of the boil, depending on the beer style. Early additions contribute to bitterness, while later ones add aroma.

3.5. Cooling and Fermentation

Post boiling, the wort needs rapid cooling to a temperature safe for the yeast (around 68-72F for ales, 45-55F for lagers). During cooling, aeration of the wort is necessary for yeast health.

With the wort cooled, yeast is added or 'pitched' into the fermentor. Over the course of several days to a week, the yeast consumes the sugars in the wort, producing alcohol, carbon dioxide, and heat. This process is known as 'primary fermentation.'

3.6. Maturation and Carbonation

After primary fermentation is complete, the beer is transferred to a secondary vessel, leaving behind spent yeast and other residues. This secondary fermentation stage is also the maturation period when beer develops its full flavor profile.

At this stage, additional carbonation can occur by allowing the yeast to ferment a little bit more sugar or by forcing carbon dioxide into the beer.

3.7. Filtration, Carbonation, and Packaging

Finally, the beer is usually filtered to remove any remaining solids, carbonated to the desired level, and then packaged into bottles, cans, or kegs for sale and distribution. It's now ready for beer enthusiasts to enjoy it.

3.8. Brewing Safety Measures

Brewing beer is essentially a chemical experiment, and like every experiment, it involves some risks. These primarily entail the risk of contamination, explosion due to pressurized gases, and injuries from boiling liquids. Make sure to maintain a clean workspace, use sanitized equipment, and always exercise caution when working with hot liquids and pressurized fermentation vessels.

Understanding the brewing process and gaining hands-on experience is the best way to learn brewing nuances and artistry. As exciting as brewing can be, always remember – it's as much a science as it is an art. Honing skills takes patience, passion, and practice. Happy brewing!

(Note: Please secure all necessary permits and abide by all local, state, and federal laws and regulations before brewing commercially.)

Chapter 4. Setting up your Microbrewery: A Step-by-step Guide

Before setting out on your brewing journey, remember this: knowledge is power. The more informed and prepared you are, the better placed you'll be to tackle this head-on and create that successful microbrewery you dream of. The aim of this guide is to lay down a comprehensive blueprint to help you transform your ale-inspired fantasies into tangible, frothy reality.

4.1. The Groundwork: Research and Understanding

Start your brewing endeavour by immersing yourself in the vast world of craft beers. Knowing what you're dipping into significantly helps in understanding the variety, brewing techniques, taste profiles, and the preferences of regular craft beer consumers. Try as many styles as possible, go to craft beer expos, listen to podcasts, read books about craft beer and brewing, visit other craft breweries if possible and talk to brewers and craft beer enthusiasts.

A key part of your research should be assessing local demand, getting to know your potential competitors, and understanding the preferences and habits of local craft beer drinkers. These insights will provide valuable data to craft your strategies ahead.

4.2. The Business Plan

Once you possess a solid foundation of knowledge, it's time to move onto structuring your thoughts and plans into a concrete business plan. This document should contain a detailed description of your business, your target market, an overview of your competitors, marketing and sales strategies, and a full financial forecast. It should clearly articulate your vision and ambition - what do you intend to bring to the existing beer market, and how? Remember, a well-structured business plan will not only serve as a roadmap for your microbrewery but will also be an essential tool when seeking financial support or investors.

4.3. Legalities and Requirements

You must acquaint yourself with the legal landscape you'll be operating within before you set up your microbrewery. This includes understanding the permits and licenses required, zoning laws, food and beverages regulations, and local health and safety guidelines. You may need specific permits for brewing, for selling alcohol, for serving food, and for holding events on your premises, among others. Hiring a lawyer specializing in the field can guide you on this path and save you from unwelcome surprises down the line.

4.4. Location Matters

The location of your brewery has a significant impact on its visibility, accessibility and operational costs. Things to keep in mind while choosing a location are the abundance of the necessary utilities such as water supply and waste disposal systems, proximity to your potential customer base, cost of warehousing if needed, and space for prospective expansion.

4.5. Brew Equipment

An investment in professional brewing equipment is recommended for serious brewers. The cost will vary substantially based on the capacity and type of brewery you wish to set up. Brew kettles, fermenters, grinders, cooling systems, storage and serving tanks, cleaning appliances, and kegging systems are some of the core equipment involved. This segment should be planned meticulously, as it forms one of the largest costs in your budget.

4.6. Recipe Development

Quality beers start with quality recipes. After lots of research, experimentation, and tasting, you should ideally have a line-up of beers ready to launch before you open your doors to the public. In addition, understanding different beer styles and mastering adjustments to reach the required taste profile needs regular practice and tweaks.

4.7. Staffing and Operations

This section covers two aspects: the operational process of brewing itself, and recruiting experienced or at least, interested staff to do the brewing. You will need people to manage inventory, brewing and fermenting, bottling, and the serving of beers. A brewery, after all, is more than a factory: it's a place of social gathering.

4.8. Marketing Strategy

A strong brand identity and compelling marketing strategy can help your craft beers stand out in an already noisy, competitive market. From the name and logo of the microbrewery to the names of your beers, from the website to the social media presence, from on-site events to inclusion in local festivals and expos - these all forms a part of your marketing strategy.

With your vision, passion, and our guide, you are now equipped to leave the shore and ride those malty waves. Remember, brewing is a remarkably labour-intensive process, and opening a brewery is not a guaranteed highway to riches. Yet, it's an exhilarating voyage, and as you stay true to quality and creativity, the rewards are plentiful. Craft beer is not only an industry but also a community. Welcome to the club, and here's to you: the newest craft brewer in town.

Chapter 5. Sourcing Quality Ingredients: From Hops to Barley

The journey of beer from grain to glass begins with the sourcing of quality ingredients. Just as a chef painstakingly sources the best produce to craft a culinary masterpiece, a brewer's quest for perfection starts with the procurement of top-tier hops, malt, yeast, and water. These core ingredients, when meticulously chosen and paired, can create a symphony of flavors that make your craft beer truly unique.

5.1. Hops

Hops are the green, cone-shaped flowers of the humulus lupulus plant and are used primarily for imparting bitterness, flavor, and aroma to the beer. They provide the counterpoint to the sweet maltiness derived from barley, and help to preserve the beer.

To buy hops, start by identifying the varieties that align with the beer style you're planning to brew. Some common varieties include Cascade for American-style ales, Saaz for pilsners, and Fuggles for English ales. Each hop variety brings with it a unique profile, ranging from floral and citrusy, to piney, earthy, and spicy.

Here's a quick guide on hop varieties:

Hop Variety	Characteristics	Best For
Cascade	Floral, Grapefruit-like	American Ales
Saaz	Spicy, Herbal	Pilsners
Fuggles	Earthy, Woody	English Ales

When sourcing, look for freshness. Hops should have strong aromas and be free of mold or discoloration. It's all about establishing strong relationships with suppliers to guarantee the best quality. It may benefit you to have contracts with suppliers, ensuring consistent availability of desired hop varieties.

5.2. Barley

Barley is the backbone of beer, providing the fermentable sugars necessary for yeast activity. Additionally, it contributes significantly to the flavor, color, and body of the beer.

Like hops, there are several varieties of barley to choose from, the most commonly used in brewing being two-row and six-row barley. Two-row barley is popular for its higher extract yield and lower protein content, while six-row barley is notorious for its high enzyme content, beneficial when using adjunct grains.

Quality barley should be plump, with a smooth surface and no signs of disease or pest damage — characteristics that reputable malt houses ensure.

5.3. Malting

Most brewers buy malted barley, which has been sprouted and dried in a controlled manner to activate enzymes necessary for brewing. However, malting isn't a mere binary process, and the degree of malting can significantly influence the beer's flavor.

For instance, lightly malted barley (Pilsner malt) gives a delicate, pale color and a gentle malty sweetness. In contrast, heavily malted barley (Chocolate malt) provides a dark hue and rich, chocolate-y flavor.

5.4. Yeast

Alcohol wouldn't exist without yeast, the magical microorganisms that consume malt sugars, producing alcohol and CO2 in the process. However, different strains of yeast also contribute a myriad of flavors and aromas, called yeast esters.

Ale yeasts are typically top-fermenting, functioning at warmer temperatures, while lager yeasts are bottom-fermenting and prefer colder conditions.

Brewers should only use fresh, uncontaminated yeast cultures to ensure consistent fermentation. Commercial yeast suppliers provide a wealth of options, and some even offer custom propagation services for specific yeast strains.

5.5. Water

Water might not seem a critical ingredient on face value, but it makes up 90-95% of most beers. The mineral content of your brewing water can significantly influence your beer's taste.

Hard water, high in calcium and magnesium ions, tends to soften hop bitterness, making it well-suited to brewing lagers and pale ales. In contrast, soft water, with low mineral content, accentuates hop bitterness and is ideal for brewing stouts and bocks.

Several companies specialize in water testing and can provide detailed analysis of your water's chemical makeup, helping you adjust your water profile for different beer styles.

Sourcing quality ingredients is a continuous, careful process demanding attention to detail. It's about building relationships with suppliers, conducting rigorous quality checks, and understanding that every ingredient, no matter how small, has a role to play in crafting that perfect brew. It's a labor of love, and when done right, it's the secret behind every successful microbrewery. Let this ethos guide you in your journey of turning hoppy dreams into frothy realities.

Chapter 6. Crafting Your Unique Beer Recipe

Creating a unique beer recipe is often seen as the beating heart of your microbrewery. It's where chemistry meets creativity, producing a unique flavor profile that will ultimately become your brewery's signature. This process involves understanding your primary ingredients, fermentation, conditioning, and ultimately, tasting and refining your product.

6.1. Understanding Your Ingredients

There are four key ingredients in beer: water, malt, hops, and yeast. Each plays a crucial role in influencing the final taste, aroma and appearance of your brew.

Water makes up about 90% of beer. The mineral content of your water can drastically influence the taste of your beer. Different water profiles are more suited to certain styles of beer - for example, hard water is typically associated with stout styles due to the rich, robust flavors it imparts.

Malt is key to the color and flavor of the beer. It provides the sugars needed for fermentation, with darker malts often contributing to a stronger flavor and a darker color.

Hops are responsible for adding bitterness to balance out the sweetness of the malt. They also contribute to the aroma. They can be added at various points during boiling; the earlier the addition, the more bitterness they add. Later additions can enhance the hop aroma without increasing bitterness.

Finally, yeast consumes the sugar from the malt, producing alcohol and carbon dioxide. Yeast also adds flavor and aroma, with different strains providing different results.

6.2. The Brewing Process

To ready your malt, you'll need to steep it in hot water in a process known as mashing. Once steeped, you heat the mixture – now called wort – and add your hops. The type, quantity, and timing of your hops will depend on the flavor profile you're aiming for. After this boiling stage, you'll need to cool the wort rapidly before adding your yeast. This yeast will turn the sugars in the wort into alcohol during fermentation.

6.3. Fermentation and Conditioning

Fermentation typically takes around two weeks. During this time, it's best to store your beer in a dark place at a stable temperature. The specific temperature will depend on the yeast strain you're using. Once fermentation is complete, you'll transfer your beer to a new container to let it condition. Conditioning helps to mellow any harsh flavors and allows sediment to settle out of the beer.

6.4. Fine-tuning Your Recipe

After the conditioning period, you can gather your team or trusted tasters to evaluate your beer. Assess the flavor, aroma, color, and mouthfeel. Does it achieve what you set out to create? What could be improved? Tweak your recipe based on the feedback you receive. This could involve adjusting the type and quantity of your ingredients, changing the fermentation temperature, or modifying the way you add hops.

6.5. Creating a Diverse Range

As your brewery grows, a varied range of beers will help attract a broader clientele. Researching other popular and successful beers can provide invaluable insights. Explore unique ingredients to differentiate your product. Remember, building a successful beer line is as much science as it is art and involves iterative experimentation.

6.6. Navigating Consistency versus Creativity

While creating new beers and flavors is exciting, remember the importance of consistency. Regular patrons will appreciate the reliability of a beer they enjoy. As such, ensure you meticulously record all recipe details, alterations, and results.

To balance creativity with consistency, having several 'core beers' that are always available while also offering seasonal or experimental beers can be an effective strategy. This approach allows brewers to satisfy both the regular drinkers and the adventurous types.

In the end, creating your unique beer recipe requires knowledge, patience, and a touch of artistry. With time and dedication, you'll develop a recipe that reflects your passion, quality, and craftmanship, creating a product your clientele will appreciate and enjoy.

Chapter 7. Mastering Brewing Techniques: A Deep Dive

The art of brewing craft beer is complex and nuanced, full of exciting possibilities and unique challenges. Learning to master the intricacies of brewing techniques is the first and most fundamental step on the path to opening your very own microbrewery. These methods can be as varied and diverse as the beer styles available, and just as vast.

7.1. Understanding Beer Ingredients

To master brewing techniques, one must first understand the basic ingredients that constitute beer: water, malt, hops, and yeast.

Water makes up about 90% to 95% of beer. The mineral content of water influences how the other ingredients interact and develop throughout the brewing process.

Malt is the source of the sugars (primarily maltose) that the yeast will consume during the fermentation process. There are two main types of malt, base malt, and specialty malt.

Hops are added to the boil for bitterness, flavor, and aroma. The alpha acids within the hops are released over time, providing the bitter counterpoint to the malt's sweetness.

Yeast is a microorganism that eats the sugars produced by the malt, converts them into alcohol, carbon dioxide, and numerous flavor compounds that establish a beer's flavor.

7.2. Grain Milling

Milling is the first physical interaction the brewer will have with their ingredients on brewing day. It's where malted grains are crushed, not ground, in a mill to open up the kernel and expose the starchy center. Home brewers usually employ a specialized grain mill that runs manually or with a drill motor.

7.3. Mashing

Mashing refers to the process of combining the milled malted grain with hot water. It is an essential process in brewing as it converts the complex carbohydrates in the malted grain into simple sugars that the yeast can consume during fermentation. The sugar-rich liquid resulting from mashing is called wort. Now, there are different mash methods like single infusion mash which is easier for newcomers, and the more complex step-mashes.

7.4. Lautering

Lautering is the art of separating the spent grains from the wort, a process vital to ensuring a good quality base for your beer. Batch sparging and fly sparging are two commonly used techniques. Largely dependent on the type of brewing method, brewers should strive to strike a balance between fast separation and obtaining as much wort as possible.

7.5. The Boil

A crucial step where you boil the wort, sterilizing it, and getting rid of unwanted proteins. This step is also where you add hops and any additional ingredients. The timing and type of hops added during the boil can considerably affect bitterness, flavor, and aroma in your final product.

7.6. Fermentation

This is where the 'magic' of brewing happens. The cooled wort is transferred to a fermentation vessel and yeast is introduced. The yeast feeds off the sugars in the wort, converting them into alcohol, CO_2 and several other compounds that give beer its flavor. The temperature and duration of the fermentation process, along with the yeast strain, closely dictate the type of beer you end up with.

7.7. Conditioning

Also known as secondary fermentation, this is the period of time the beer needs to rest, mature and clarify. The beer is transferred to a second fermenter to rid any collected yeast or sediment. It is during this step that any remaining yeast continues to act on the beer, smoothing out any harsh flavors in the process.

Mastering brewing techniques imply mastering scientific rigor, creativity, and consistency. Each brew is a test, a learning opportunity, and a step on the journey to fulfilling your craft beer dreams. The nuances of each step, from grain to glass, all contribute to the final flavors, aromas, and characteristics your beer will embody.

Remember, brewing should be about exploring, innovating, and pushing at the boundaries of what is possible in a pint. So get out there, brew something truly remarkable, and let your brewing journey begin!

Chapter 8. Marketing Your Craft Beer: Strategies for Success

Craft beer is about unique tastes and craftsmanship. Yet, no matter the quality of your brew, it won't bring you profit if it doesn't reach consumers' glasses. Marketing is your key to unlock that door. Before getting started, familiarize yourself with the two main aspects of marketing: the strategic and the tactical. While the strategic focuses on identifying your target audience and tailoring your product accordingly, the tactical executes the action of bringing your beer closer to this audience through promotional events, social media, collaboration, etc.

8.1. Understanding Your Target Audience

Craft beer drinkers are not a single homogeneous group. They come with different tastes, cultural backgrounds, and income levels. Thus, understanding these consumers paves the way to your marketing success. Make use of demographics and psychographics to find your most promising audience.

Demographics refer to aspects such as age, gender, income, education, and location. Generally, craft beer drinkers tend to be between 25 to 50 years old and lean slightly male, with at least some college education.

Psychographics, on the other hand, delve into consumers' personality, interests, and lifestyle. Craft beer enthusiasts are often curious, up for trying new things, and value craftsmanship and uniqueness. They're likely to participate in community events and engage on social media about their favorite beers.

Always remember: understanding your target audience doesn't mean excluding others, but rather knowing where to direct your main marketing efforts.

8.2. Picturing Your Brand

Now that you have an idea of who your audience is, it's time to project your brand in a way that resonates with them. Your brand is your business personality, and it extends far beyond your logo or tagline.

Take time to create a brand that aligns with your vision and values. Be consistent with your brand across all platforms and products, whether that's your beer label designs, website, or social media posts. The key is to make your brand relatable and easily recognizable.

Portraying a compelling backstory about your brewery also aids in deepening the connection with consumers. It could be about the inspiration behind your brewing, your commitment to the local community, or your dedication to sustainable practices.

8.3. Utilizing Social Media

Social media is a cost-effective and powerful tool for your marketing needs. Create engaging content that tells a story - your brand's story. Highlight the brewing process, introduce your team, share customer testimonials, or announce upcoming events. This helps build a community of loyal followers.

Websites such as Untappd and RateBeer are popular among craft beer fans for rating and discovering beers. Make sure your brews are listed to enhance visibility and obtain feedback.

8.4. Collaboration and Co-branding

Working with other breweries, restaurants, or local businesses broadens your reach and creates unique marketing opportunities. You may brew a special beer together with another brewery or create a dedicated beer for a local restaurant. These collaborations bring freshness to your offerings and allure more consumers.

8.5. Craft Beer Festivals and Events

These events provide a platform to showcase your beers to a wider audience. Attendees are already interested in craft beer and are eager to try new brews. Prepare engaging presentations and stand out from the crowd.

8.6. Creatively Packaging Your Beer

Invest in high-quality, attractive packaging that speaks volumes about your brand and catches consumers' eyes on crowded store shelves. Equally important are clear and informative labels that disclose the beer style, ABV%, brewing date, and batch number, giving customers all the necessary information.

8.7. Establishing a Brewery Taproom

Brewery taprooms serve multiple functions: taste-testing lab, direct sales outlet, and brand ambassador. It's the place where you can display your complete beer collection, host events, and interact directly with consumers.

8.8. Navigating the Legal Landscape

Marketing beer comes with certain legal considerations. Make sure to familiarize yourself with both federal and state laws regarding labeling, advertising, and social media. Consult a professional if in doubt, to prevent any legal hiccups in your marketing plan.

In conclusion, marketing in the craft beer industry is about much more than selling beer. It's about building a story and a community around your brand. It's about passion transferred from your brewing kettle into the hearts of beer enthusiasts. Craft carefully, market creatively!

Chapter 9. Navigating Legal and Regulatory Waters in the Beer Industry

Crafting beer is a wonderful blending of science, nature, and art, but before one hops headfirst into the brewing process, one must understand the legal landscape. The brewing industry, including craft beer, is regulated both nationally and locally. In essence, every beer you brew and sell will swim through a variety of legal and regulatory waters.

9.1. Understanding Federal Regulations

The primary federal agency tasked with regulating the alcohol industry in the United States is the Alcohol and Tobacco Tax and Trade Bureau (TTB). Part of the Department of the Treasury, the TTB oversees tax collection on alcoholic beverages, ensures fair trade practice, and enforces labeling and advertising laws.

Your first step in regulatory compliance is to obtain a Brewer's Notice from TTB. This process asks for biographical information, evidence of brewery's premises, detailed blueprint of the facility, equipment used, fermentation process, security measures, and all product sources.

Besides notice paperwork, you must also address: - Recordkeeping: Maintain accurate and comprehensive records regarding production, storage, and distribution. - Reporting: Submit recurring (monthly or quarterly) operational reports. - Tax: Pay federal excise taxes on beer production.

For labeling, all bottles must have a government-approved label with details like brand name, type of beer, alcohol content, net contents, and manufacturer's name and address.

Advertising, also under federal purview, stipulates that television, radio, print or outdoor advertising must always clearly identify the product as beer and must also contain mandatory health warning statements.

9.2. State and Local Regulations

Apart from federal laws, states too have their own regulatory framework. These laws differ significantly, making it crucial to understand the particular rules in the state where your brewery will operate. Some states require a brewer to work with a wholesaler, limiting direct sales, while others may allow self-distribution.

Check with your local Alcohol and Beverage Control Board for specific laws on advertising, distribution, labeling, and point of sale. Remember, licensed breweries may need additional state and local permits, such as food and health licenses, if serving food products on-site.

Application procedures, processing times, costs, and renewals also vary from state to state. Be prepared for these processes to take time, hence starting on time is advisable.

9.3. Working with Wholesale Distributors

In many US states, alcohol distribution follows the 'Three-Tier System': manufacturers, wholesalers, and retailers. By law, brewers sell to licensed wholesalers, who in turn sell to retailers.

If the laws of your state require you to work through a distributor, select one that understands your brand, clientele, and business ethos. It is a crucial decision as the distributor is the link between you and your final consumers.

9.4. Brewery Operations

Regulations do not cease with the approval of your brewing license. Safety is paramount in brewery operations, as these involve the use of heavy machinery, hot fluids, pressurized systems, chemicals, and more.

You must meet state and local safety guidelines, like using approved equipment, providing Personal Protective Equipment to employees, and strictly adhering to sanitization practices.

Fire safety regulations are also important given the potential fire hazards associated with brewing operations.

9.5. The Role of Legal Counsel

Finally, due to the complex and diverse legal and regulatory landscape, working with a legal professional specializing in the alcohol industry is highly recommended. They guide in contract law, licensing, intellectual property issues, and litigation possibilities. Ensuring you're legally compliant can save you a great deal of time, money, and stumbling into unnecessary legal predicaments.

Entering the craft beer scene requires more than just creativity and brewing prowess. It's a journey filled with legal and regulatory hurdles that requires excellent planning. As you wade through the legal waters, remember to celebrate the small victories, seeking the counsel you need, and always keep the joy of crafting unique beers at the heart of your fledgling microbrewery. Above all, maintain compliance with all legal requirements and develop clear, ethical practices and you'll create a respected and successful venture in the craft beer industry.

Chapter 10. Building a Robust Distribution Network

A robust distribution network is critical to the success of your microbrewery. It determines how efficiently and reliably your products reach the market. Figuring out who will sell your beer, where and how will help you strategize your production and brewing schedules with greater accuracy.

10.1. Understanding the Three-Tier System

The United States follows a three-tier system of beer distribution, which has its roots in the aftermath of Prohibition. This system includes brewers, distributors or wholesalers, and retailers. It was designed to avoid over-consumption by creating a system of checks and balances.

While this system brings certain restrictions, it also provides some shields for smaller breweries, ensuring large breweries cannot monopolize the market. Despite the existence of this system, individual states laws differ, and it's important to understand the specifics for your locale.

10.2. Developing a Distribution Strategy

The first decision you'll have to make is whether to self-distribute or work with a distributor. Self-distribution allows you to have more control; however, it can be labor-intensive and requires additional permits. Working with a distributor gives you access to a wider market but comes with its challenges, like less control over how and where your beer is sold.

10.3. Self-Distribution Considerations

If you choose to travel the self-distribution route, consider the following nuances:

- *Location*: The distance between your brewery and your markets will impact delivery schedules, freshness, and cost-effectiveness.
- *Scale*: How much product you can deliver effectively and efficiently.
- *Resources*: The manpower and mode of distribution you possess or are willing to invest in.
- *Legalities*: The licensing regulations in your specific state to allow for self-distribution.

10.4. Finding the Right Distribution Partner

On the other hand, if you're considering working with a distributor, here are some questions to consider:

- *Experience*: Do they have a good history dealing with craft beers?
- *Portfolio*: Are your beers a good fit for their existing product lines?
- *Communication*: Is there a good line of communication, and do they understand your vision?
- *Sales*: Do they have a strong sales team and a healthy relationship with retailers?

10.5. Contractual Agreements: Dos and Don'ts

When formalizing a relationship with a distributor, it's important to have everything in writing. A legally drafted contract outlining all aspects of your partnership will serve as a safeguard against misunderstandings. Be sure to seek legal counsel to help with this process.

10.6. Strategies for Effective Market Penetration

Your distribution strategy must include an effective market penetration plan. Offer promotional discounts to your early retailers, invest in eye-catching POS displays to attract consumers, and never underestimate the power of in-person tasting events. Craft beer lovers often follow trends, new flavors, and the culture – so consider creating that vibe around your brand.

10.7. Navigating Challenges in the Distribution Network

As your brand and brewery grow, challenges will arise. These might include scaling your production, maintaining product quality, running out of storage space or dealing with fluctuating demand through seasons. Navigating these issues will require proactive preparation, solid planning, and open communication with your partners.

10.8. Leveraging Technology in Distribution

Technology, with all its advancements, can greatly aid your distribution strategies. Consider using an automatic route planner for efficient deliveries, a CRM for managing client interactions, inventory management systems to avoid stock-outs, and sales analytics for informed decision-making.

10.9. Review and Refine

As with all aspects of your business, your distribution strategy should be dynamic. Continually review and refine it base on the changes in the market, industry norms, and your brewery's capacity and objectives.

10.10. Conclusion

Building a robust distribution network may seem daunting, but with careful planning, it is achievable. By understanding the distribution system laws, carefully choosing your distribution method, creating comprehensive contracts, strategizing for market penetration, and using technology, you can create a distribution strategy that will ensure your craft beers are loved by many. This will help you turn your passion into a profitable (and delicious) venture.

Overall, this remains a tremendous boon for craft beer – a solid distribution channel can act as your liaison with the market, enabling your brew to flow freely, touching tastebuds far and wide, keeping your liquid artistry in high demand.

Chapter 11. Future Trends: Staying Relevant in a Dynamic Landscape

The craft beer industry, like any other, is driven by consumer preferences and trends. These range from the type of ingredients used, to the brewing process, branding, and even packaging. Moreover, with the ever-changing consumer tastes, it is vital to stay abreast of these trends to maintain and increase your brewery's relevance in the market.

11.1. The Resurgence of Traditional and Local Ingredients

Recent years have seen a growing interest in traditional and local ingredients. This trend is driven by consumers' desire for unique, authentic experiences. Brewers have started experimenting with local flavors, trying to capture the terroir in their brews. Ingredients such as locally sourced grains, yeasts, and even foraged botanicals are finding their way into craft beers. Embracing local ingredients not only enhances flavors but also contributes to sustainability, which is another significant trend in the industry.

11.2. Sustainability and Eco-friendly Initiatives

The world is becoming more conscious of its footprint, and there is an increasing emphasis on green and sustainable practices, including in the brewing industry. Brewers are exploring various ways to implement more eco-friendly practices, such as using renewable energy to power their operations or recycling byproducts. Some breweries are even adopting a 'zero waste' goal, turning their spent grains into cattle feed or using it for baking bread.

Customers today are more conscious about the businesses they support, preferring those that align with their values. Thus, promoting your microbrewery's eco-friendly initiatives can be a significant part of your brand story and a way to gain market share.

11.3. Innovation in Flavors

Flavors in the world of craft beer are ever-evolving. Brewers are becoming more adventurous, stepping out of the traditional beer flavor boundaries. We have seen a surge in fruit-infused beers, beer-wine hybrids, and beers with unexpected flavors like chili, chocolate, and spices. Similarly, non-alcoholic craft beers are gaining ground, championed by those who enjoy the flavors of craft beer, but wish to limit their alcohol consumption.

Staying updated on these trends and experimenting with new flavors on a small scale can help you distinguish your microbrewery.

11.4. Digital Technologies and Online Presence

In this digital age, maintaining an effective online presence will be a key to staying relevant. Apart from having a high-quality website and engaging social media profiles, consider leveraging newer technologies as well. For instance, virtual tours of your microbrewery could offer a unique experience to potential customers.

Online sales and deliveries are another aspect to consider seriously. The pandemic has resulted in a paradigm shift, with consumers increasingly opting for home deliveries, a trend that seems here to stay.

11.5. Collaboration and Community Engagement

Collaboration is a potent trend in the craft beer industry. Breweries are coming together to create unique, limited-edition collaboration beers. Apart from creating a unique product, such collaborations can result in a wider reach, tapping into the customer base of the collaborating breweries.

Similarly, fostering a strong sense of community can go a long way in building brand loyalty. Regularly hosting events, taking part in local activities, or even simply providing a warm, welcoming space where people can gather, can help establish a strong local presence.

To sum up, staying relevant in the dynamic landscape of the craft beer industry will require keen observation of the preferences of your target audience and flexibility to adapt to those trends. It is about striking a sound balance between retaining the essence of your brand and evolving with market trends. The future of the craft beer industry seems to be promising, filled with exciting new flavors, sustainable practices, and a stronger connection with the local communities. Staying attuned to these changes will ensure that your microbrewery can ride the wave of growth successfully.